MW00568649

THE
AVERY
COLLECTION

By W. H. Peckitt

THE AVERY
COLLECTION.

THE

AVERY COLLECTION

OF THE

POSTAGE STAMPS OF
THE WORLD

BY

W. H. PECKITT

LONDON
W. H. PECKITT, 47 STRAND, W.C.

———

1909

A766715

Sir WILLIAM B. AVERY, Bart.

Preface.

IN the period at which it was formed the famous Avery Collection was second only to that of the Tapling Collection of Stamps in Great Britain It has much in common with the great collection which now reposes in the British Museum, in that it is a vast, comprehensive, general collection of the stamps of the entire world, and it covers exactly the same period—from the beginning until 1890

As this is the first collection of such national philatelic importance that has yet been broken up, it seemed to me that collectors both at home and abroad would be glad to have a souvenir of this great event, and the form which naturally presented itself to me as the most likely to be of interest and of service to collectors was a short account of the collection, accompanied by some illustrations of its truly wonderful contents

I was glad to have the opportunity of acquiring this collection, for I had the privilege of being a friend of the late owner, and had had no small share in procuring for him many of the choicest treasures it contains All these are in the collection to this day, and many of them are gems which nowadays are only to be acquired in really important collections of the olden time.

Such a collection makes a very appreciable addition to one's stock, and, besides supplementing my resources in the old issues of British and British Colonial stamps, it greatly strengthens my stock of the stamps of foreign countries The contents of my books of these latter issues have been greatly absorbed, and the replenishing of them happily coincides with the increasing popularity of foreign issues among collectors.

The transaction by which I was enabled to acquire the Avery Collection is the largest cash purchase on record in connection with the pastime of stamp collecting, the amount of £24,500 being paid by me to the executors in a single cheque, being also probably one of the most extensive deals in any form of collecting hobby

Contents.

Sir William B Avery
as a Philatelist

As a stamp collector Sir William started at a very early age. In a letter to a mutual friend about "this charming and interesting hobby," he wrote :

"I began when I was eight years old, and collected in a very rough and elementary way until I was about seventeen years old, having a collection of about 1500-1600 stamps when I sold my collection in 1871

"I did nothing more in stamps until about 1878 when I commenced again with Lincoln's album, and was fortunate enough to fill up most of the blank spaces, and had a very good number of rare stamps I was however, very disgusted with this style of collecting when I paid a visit to the Birmingham Philatelic Society and saw the method of arranging stamps on hinges and classifying perforations, and I finally decided, about 1887, to sell my collection again

"I sold some portion, but as I saw some of the rarities go I changed my mind and began again with a good Senf album As I filled up one country after another I began removing these into special albums

"I had the opportunity of buying a good special collection of Australian stamps belonging to Mr Bullock, of Australia, and added the Australian stamps I had before to these, and so made it into a much stronger and more perfect collection.

"Since then I have specialised Ceylon, India, all English Colonies, Switzerland, France, and several countries in North and South America and Africa, and have altogether between 90,000 and 100,000 stamps Most of them are used and unused.

"In the early days I often felt most discouraged when I saw really fine collections of specialities, but I persevered, and as the saying is quite true, ' most things come to those who know how to wait,' I am glad to say by waiting and patiently working I have now got many stamps which at one time I thought it would be impossible for me ever to attain "

Sir William thus told the outline of the story of his collecting experiences. I need only add that his collection and his time were very generously placed at the service of many philatelic societies, and his name on the programme of a meeting invariably ensured a crowded attendance. At philatelic exhibitions he was no less generous His name does not appear in the catalogue of the London 1890 International Exhibition, but in 1897 he made a gigantic show, though he considerately marked his displays as "not for competition "

There he displayed his magnificent Mauritius for the first time at a public exhibition, and he had the field here all to himself, as his was the recognised premier collection of these most valued stamps He also shewed his British Guiana, confining his grand display to the issues of 1850, 1852, 1853, 1856, and 1862, these being the most difficult for anyone else to shew, and, needless to say, this was one of the most valuable groups in the Exhibition In Australians Mr Avery shewed various colonies *in extenso* His Cape of Good Hope display, which was perhaps the most popular in the show at the galleries of the Institute of Painters in Water Colours, was limited to his extremely choice lot of triangular issues.

In the 1906 Exhibition he shewed his superb collections of Switzerland and Nevis.

On several occasions Sir William entertained parties of philatelists at his beautiful country house, Oakley Court, Windsor, and the visitors to the 1906 Exhibition will always retain pleasant memories of the delightful visit paid to Sir William Avery during the course of the last great International Exhibition

Sir William made several notable purchases during the formation of his collection. The acquisition of three complete sets of the first issue of Moldavia in one transaction is, I think, without a parallel in the annals of our hobby. In addition to the Bullock Collection of Australians mentioned in the letter quoted above, he purchased the Blest Collection, which was a fine general one of British Colonials, but was particularly strong in stamps of the West Indies, and the Mackenzie Collection of Nevis The Blest Collection, I believe, cost Sir William about £5000 He also bought Lieutenant Napier's specialised Collection of Greece

Then he had the pick of most of the big collections that came on the market for many years past, and many of his choicest gems came from such collections as Mr. Hastings J Wright's "Great Britain," Ehrenbach's "German Empire," and many others

I now proceed to an account of some of the beauties of this remarkable collection, starting with the stamps of Great Britain and her overseas Empire.

In describing some of the rarities, I would ask the reader's indulgence, inasmuch as it is a matter of considerable difficulty, where so many of the great rarities are in such a wonderful state of perfection, to find varied and adequate terms for description

Also, in order to bring this souvenir within convenient limits it has been quite impossible to refer to more than a few specially interesting items in most of the countries referred to. The omission of a country, or the omission of any reference to particular stamps, should not be taken to infer that they are absent from the collection, but that exigencies of space have led me to omit mention of stamps which are in most cases quite fully represented, but do not present really exceptional features

The Avery Collection

Part I —Great Britain and Colonies

PRICE 1^d Per Label, 1^s Per Row of 12, £1...

Great Britain : The 1d. V.R. Black stamps.

GREAT BRITAIN

I might here mention that most of the finest English stamps came from the Hastings Wright Collection, and were bought in 1895 Many of the rarities are in a condition which is not to be equalled in any collection of later times

As we open the volume set apart for the stamps of this country, we find the collection makes a very appropriate commencement with the Parliamentary envelopes which are referred to in Rowland Hill's diary under the date January 13, 1840 Following upon a visit of Hill to the Speaker of the House of Commons, there were issued on January 16 "letter covers" which the members could buy at the office for the sale of Parliamentary papers These letter covers were to pass free through the Post Office, and were the immediate predecessors of the Mulready envelope and the adhesive postage stamp

There were several varieties of these interesting covers, and the collection under review contains two copies of the House of Commons variety, one of the Houses of Parliament envelopes, and two of the House of Lords, one of the latter being on yellow and the other on blue paper.

Mulready's envelopes and covers are represented by ordinary specimens and a proof on India paper

Among the 1d blacks the most notable items are the 1d. V.R stamps in a single, a pair, and a magnificent block of twenty.

The introduction of perforating, as every collector knows, was the result of experiments made by Mr Henry Archer, and one of his experimental "roulettes" is included in the collection

There are also the 1d on Dickinson paper; the
1d red, imperforate, in a block of 40; and four unused
singles of plate 225.

Of the line-engraved 1½d. stamp copies are included
imperforate and with the error OP-PC, and there is a
grand block of forty imperforate, in the issued colour,
and shewing the error.   Other large pieces are
included of the lilac-rose, including a block of fifteen

Of the 2d " no lines " there are two unused pairs
and three singles   There is also a large block (32) of
the imperforate 2d. with white lines.

The 3d " secret dot " is shewn with unofficial
perforation, and a complete unbroken pane shewing
the sheet number " 20."

The 4d " small garter " is included, perforated and
imperforate, unused , the " medium garter " on blue
paper, and a pair of mediums on white paper ; and a
block of the " large garter " in the first printing

The embossed stamps are all in an unequalled state
of preservation; there is the 6d. in a magnificent right-
hand corner block of four   Another specimen of the
6d. is, without doubt, the finest copy known, its
embossing being bold and absolutely unsullied

Coming to the surface-printed 6d., we find the
" hair lines," imperforate, in a pane of twenty, shewing
sheet number " 212," and the 6d overprint with only
one dot under the superior letter " 6ᵈ ".

The 9d , plate 5, which came from the Wright
Collection, is an extreme rarity.   Only seven or eight
copies of this stamp are known.

Of the 10d. embossed there are superb copies,
including unused block of four in mint state and a
strip of three (no die number) from the right-hand top
corner of the sheet.   There is also a vertical pair, one

stamp overlapping the other quite half-way up the first impressed stamp

The 1/- embossed are as fine, the die number standing up on the copies as fresh as if the stamps were just off the embossing machine Several of these are out of the Wright Collection.

The 1/- violet (surface printed) is shewn perforated and imperforate.

Of the 2/- blue there are pairs perforated and imperforate, and the 2/- brown in a nice pair, unused.

The 5/-, 10/-, and £1, watermarked Cross, are all here, and the 10/- blue on blued paper in fine unused state

The £1, watermarked "Three Crowns" and "Three Orbs," are shewn in very fine state and with shades, and there is the £5 on blued paper Of the I R officials there are three pairs of the 5/- and 10/- , the 5/- on blued paper , the £1 brown, watermarked "Crowns" and ' Orbs " , and two of the £1 green.

BARBADOS.

Among the better known rarities here there is the 1d on half 5/-, unused. Of the Large Star watermarks there is a block of six of the 1s , fifty of the ½d. grass-green, ten 1/-, no watermark, and four each of the 6d and 1/-, imperforate

BRITISH COLUMBIA AND VANCOUVER ISLAND

The few stamps of this colony are complete, and there are several copies of most of the values.

BRITISH GUIANA

Here we have one of the colonies whose stamps provide one of the broad fields in which the philatelic giants roam among rarities Sir William had most

of the gems of this colony, including the famous
circular 2 cents rose, which is one of the most highly
esteemed of philatelic treasures Unfortunately, Sir
William sold this stamp to me some years ago, and it
is not now in the collection His reason for parting
with it was that it was not a very fine specimen and
he had hoped to get a finer one, a hope that,
alas, was never to be realised.

The other very rare circular stamps of 1850 are
represented by the 4 cents on orange and on yellow
paper, two 8 cents on green, and five 12 cents on blue,
and the 4 cents on yellow on pelure paper. The variety
of the 12 cents in which the 2 has a straight foot is
included This, of course, is a rarity doubly rare

Of the long, upright, oblong stamps of 1852, lithographed by Waterlow of London, there is one 1 cent
black on magenta, unused, a block of four, and seven
singles, used Of the 4 cents black on deep blue there
are two unused and five used

The next issue (1853) is another series of fine
stamps represented in the collection by some grand
copies unused, and showing the types Of the 1 cent
there are six unused, and pairs and strips, and a strip
of five shewing the types used. Of the 4 cents blue
there are four unused without the white line and two
with the white line.

In the next set, printed in the office of the *Official
Gazette*, at Georgetown, in February, 1856, the 1 cent
black on magenta is one of the few great rarities which
is missing from the Avery Collection As every
collector knows, only one copy of this stamp is known,
and that is the specimen in the collection of M la
Renotière Of the companion rarity, however, the
collection contains one of the 4 cents, on blue surface-
coloured paper, and four singles and two on entire
original envelope of the 4 cents on magenta.

British Guiana, 1862.
4 cents. black on blue.
One of the three known sheets.

The subsequent Waterlow issue is shewn in prolific display, but I will pass these and come to the type-set stamps printed by Mr. George Melville, of the *Royal Gazette*, in 1862

Of the 1 cent black on rose there is a complete sheet unsigned   The stamps are usually initialled with the letters R.M (Robert Mather, the Acting Receiver General of the Colony)   There are also three unused signed copies and numerous used specimens

A sheet of the 2 cents black on yellow has been reconstructed, partly from unused and partly from used copies and there are also some duplicates

The 4 cents black on blue, which is very much rarer than the 1 cent, is here in a complete reconstructed setting, including seventeen unused and unsigned copies, sixteen of which are in one block There are, I believe, only three such settings known, one being in the British Museum, one in the collection of M. la Renotière, and this is the third, of which I give an illustration from the Avery Collection

British Honduras

A good collection, right up to the end of the Queen's head issue of 1899, and including the 3 cents on 3d brown, perforated 12½.

CANADA.

This is a particularly good album, containing five of the rare 12d. black. Of these two are in a magnificent unused pair, another is a superb unused single copy, with large side margin in perfectly fresh state of colour, and probably a first impression. Two of the five copies are used.

Other choice stamps are the 6d. on thick paper, unused, six of the 6d., imperforate, unused, a pair of the 10d. and another pair of the $7\frac{1}{2}$d., all imperforate and unused, a strip of four $7\frac{1}{2}$d. green, and six of the 6d., perforated 12.

CAPE OF GOOD HOPE.

"Woodblocks," block of four 1d. brick red.

The tri-cornered stamps of this colony, which have always held a high place in the esteem of all collectors, both advanced and elementary, are in a beautiful array

B

in this collection, and include most of the rare varieties.

Three fine unused copies of the 1d. brick-red on blued paper and three of the 4d. blue on blued paper make a very promising opening page to the collection

The 6d slate-lilac on blued paper is in an unused pair.

There is also the 6d lilac rouletted

The provisional issues, popularly known as " Woodblocks," comprise some magnificent copies, in singles and pairs ; in fact, the condition of the " Woodblocks " is finer even than that of these stamps in the famous Vernon Roberts' Collection, which I acquired in 1907

There are two unused 1d " woodblocks," a block of four of the 1d brick-red, unique in its perfection of condition   The 4d. is in a pair and a single unused, and five superb used pairs in different shades   Of the deep blue 4d there are twelve copies and one magnificient unused stamp   In printing these stamps from a number of separate electrotypes, one of the *cliches* of the 1d value got in with the set prepared for printing the 4d value, and one of the 4d *cliches* got amongst the 1d *cliches*   The result was that in printing the sheet of 4d blue stamps one of the 1d. *cliches* was printed in blue instead of red   Similarly, one of the 4d. ones got printed in red instead of blue.

These errors are of great rarity, and the copies of them in this collection could scarcely be surpassed in their condition   There is a very fine 1d blue, and a pair shewing the error 1d blue and the normal 4d blue *se tenant*   There are also two brilliant copies of the 4d red

Another rare stamp is the 4d with retouched right-hand corner   This is shewn in a pair with the normal stamp *se tenant*.

4d. red error.

1d. blue error with 4d. blue *se tenant*.

4d. red error.

In the later stamps are many desirable possessions. I note in particular the error "THE.EE PENCE" on 4d., in perfect mint state.

CEYLON.

Some carefully selected copies of the beautiful imperforate stamps of the first issues are in this section of the collection.   The 9d. unused is illustrated. There is a fine pair of the 1/9 unused, and two mint copies of the 2/-.   In addition, there is a fine series of used copies.   The ½d. lilac on bluish paper is represented by two unused copies, and the 2/- clean cut perforation all round is also included among the unused specimens.   Other important items are the 9d. reddish brown, unused ; a pair, used, of the 2d. yellow green watermarked Crown and CC, and a long range of the late issues including some scarce surcharge varieties.

COOK ISLANDS.

This colony, which presents a small but not uninteresting series of stamps for the moderate specialist, is extensively shewn in the collection, with some nice blocks and all the paper and perforation varieties.

FIJI.

It is only in collections formed a good many years ago by the collectors of the old school that one is

nowadays able to occasionally procure really nice lots
of authentic copies of the Fiji Times Express stamps,
and they are in the Avery Collection on a fine scale
on both the *quadrillé* and the *laid batonné* papers.

Amongst the items that attract particular attention
there are two pairs of the 3d and 9d values *se tenant*
and the 6d. and 1s. *se tenant*, a very fine lot of the
later surcharges, including a pair of the 2d. on 12 cents ,
on 6d used

India.

India presents a good showing, though there is
little that requires special notice.   There is a fine
series of the stamps issued under the authority of
Sir Henry Bartle Frere, who was Chief Commissioner
in Scinde in July, 1852   These are small, embossed
labels of a curious character, and represent the begin-
nings of the introduction of the postage stamp system
in India.   A complete sheet of the half anna stamp
of the first general Indian issue is an item in this
collection with which one very rarely meets.

Ionian Islands

Of the stamps issued in 1859 for these islands,
previous to their being ceded to Greece, 30th May,
1864, there is a very nice lot, including two of the
blue stamps and two of the yellow ones, used together
on one envelope.   This portion of the collection
contains an interesting variety of postmarks.

Madagascar.

It is unusual to find more than single copies of
these curious stamps in even important collections,
but they are represented in the Avery Collection in
strips, with many of the varieties

If one could designate any one portion of this monumental collection as being the country *par excellence* one would have to accord the palm to Mauritius, which is, at the same time, one of the most fascinating philatelic studies, and also the country which claims the most valued of gems, the " Post Office " Mauritius

The collection of these stamps was exhibited at the London International Philatelic Exhibition in 1897

Both of the famous Post Office Mauritius are in the collection. They are both superb, unused copies. These stamps are much rarer unused than used Of the twenty-six copies known of these stamps there are only five unused of the 2d. value, and only two of the 1d. unused. The Avery copy of the 1d value, and the one in the collection of M La Renotière are the only unused 1d Post Office Mauritius known.

Both of these highly-treasured stamps were found in the correspondence of a big firm in the armament business at Bordeaux They were acquired by Mrs Dubois, who had the majority of the known ' Post Offices " through her hands These two were sold to Mons. E Lalanne about 1867.

M Lalanne also acquired two used copies of the stamps In 1893, the collection Lalanne was sold to Mons Piet Lataudrie, an *avocat* of Niort, France, who, not desiring to keep the four Post Office Mauritius, commissioned Mons Marcel Pouget to sell the two beautiful unused ones for him, retaining the used ones for his collection. In this way, Sir William Avery became possessed of these incomparable copies of the best known of philatelic *rara aves*.

The matchless unused copies of the 1d. and 2d. "Post Office"
Mauritius.

The "Post Paid" error.
PENOE for PENCE.

Of the other rare early issues of Mauritius there is
a splendid range of the stamps inscribed POST PAID,
on yellow, white, and bluish papers, including choice
early impressions of the 1d., and the later impressions
in unused vertical pairs.   There are also three grand
premières gravures of the 2d., one of them an incomparable copy of the error PENOE   In addition, there
are numbers of the later impressions unused, and some
beautiful used copies, which are so lightly cancelled
that it is difficult in several cases to discern whether
they are used or unused   There are three other PENOE
errors, and a reconstructed plate of this 2d value.

Of the "small fillet' 2d there are some fine
unused and a reconstructed plate   There are two
unused and five used of the "large fillet," and, in
addition, a copy used with the dull magenta 9d of
the Britannia type, on an entire envelope

The "Greek border" set of December, 1859, is
very fine.   There are seven singles and a pair of the
1d unused, and perfect used copies in singles and pairs
Of the 2d value there are two unused, two used pairs,
and various singles.   Of the 1/- Britannia type perforated there are an unused and seven used copies.

The later issues have been collected on a similarly
fine scale.

NATAL

The earliest stamps of this colony are very rarely
seen in such "new" condition as the Avery copies,
notably the four 3d and the four 9d., three of which
are exceptionally large copies ; there are, in addition,
two of the 9d stamps used on entire original cover
There is also a copy of the 1/-, which is matchless
both for size and impression.   All the later issues and
surcharges are fine.

NEVIS.

4d. rose, complete sheet.

This island colony has always been a favourite with collectors of the old school, and the pretty little sheets of twelve, in which the quaint early types were printed, make a most attractive show in a collection. Sir William had the exceptional opportunity of purchasing the famous Mackenzie collection, which

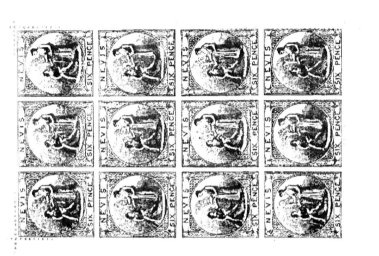

6d. lithographed, complete sheet.

1/- lithographed, engraved

had always the reputation of being the collection *par excellence* of Nevis.

The complete sheets of twelve include proof sheets of the engraved 1d. in green, 4d. in pale blue, 6d in yellow, and 1/- in rose.

Of the 1d. engraved, in addition to a large number of single specimens, there is an entire unbroken sheet of the variety on grey paper, and two plates reconstructed of unused, and one plate of used specimens

The 4d value is strongly represented There is a grand unbroken sheet in mint state, and there are two reconstructed plates of unused and one of used specimens

The 6d stamp is also shewn on much the same scale, with an unbroken mint sheet, one reconstructed sheet of unused, and one of used copies

The 1/ is shewn reconstructed, both unused and used.

Of the engraved 1d., perforated 15, there is an unbroken sheet; the 4d orange also an unbroken sheet, and one unused reconstructed sheet and one used. The 1/- blue-green is in an unbroken sheet with full margins. It is extremely rare in this condition There is also a sheet reconstructed of used specimens Of the 1/- yellow-green there are several copies, used and unused, and the laid paper rarity

The lithographed stamps of the same types are all fine There are four shades in unbroken sheets of the 1d The 4d is in an unbroken sheet, and a sheet has been reconstructed of used copies, and there are, in addition, pairs and singles unused The 6d is represented by an unbroken sheet, pairs, and twenty singles, unused There are complete sheets of the 1/- pale and 1/- deep green, and the imperforate variety in pairs. Of the 1d., perforated 11½, there are two unbroken sheets.

The later issues are very strong—the twenty 2½d. Crown C C. stamps, an array of bisected, and double surcharges in violet and black, unused, and five of the 6d. green, being the most notable items.

NEW BRUNSWICK

Of the beautiful first issue printed in London there are nineteen of the 6d and eight of the 1/- value, two of the latter being unused.

There are two of the rare Connell stamps, which, as most collectors know, were withdrawn on account of the outcry against the Postmaster-General, Charles Connell, for having the audacity to put his own portrait on one of the colony's postage stamps The "split" provisionals, consisting of the stamps of the various denominations cut in half to represent half the face value, are here shewn on the entire envelopes, including some interesting postmarks

NEWFOUNDLAND.

Here we have a rare profusion of the first type. Of the 2d. scarlet-vermilion there are ten copies, two being unused. There is also a pair with very large margins on entire envelope. This pair, which came out of the Blest Collection, is, I believe, unique

There are six 4d scarlet-vermilion, two being brilliant unused copies, five of the 6d. scarlet-vermilion, two of them unused , seven of the 6½d. scarlet-vermilion , and nine of the 1/- scarlet-vermilion, one of the latter being a beautiful unused copy.

Of the orange-vermilion specimens there are eight of the 4d., five of them unused, and one being the stamp from the bottom right-hand corner of the sheet, with margin and full gum   There are also ten of the 6d (two unused) and four of the 1/- (one unused).

The extent to which the later issues have been specialised may be hinted at by the mention of no fewer than fifty-seven copies of the 5c brown of 1866 (seal design).

NOVA SCOTIA

The 1851-1853 issue includes a splendid page of the 1d., including strips unused ; sixteen of the 6d., six of which are unused, in various shades, including a pair with original gum , eight of the 1/-, four of which are beautiful unused copies

OIL RIVERS

The stamps of this Protectorate are particularly well represented with all the varieties of surcharges The collection is especially strong in the surcharges on the De La Rue types

ST. CHRISTOPHER

This is a popular little colony with the stamp collector, who finds ample scope for a moderately-specialised collection   The whole of the issues up to the time when the special stamps for St. Christopher were superseded by the general issues for Leeward Islands in 1890 are complete

ST. HELENA

Here we have the 6d. without surcharge in nice blocks, and the 1d., imperforate, in blocks of six the other overprints forming a very beautiful lot.

ST LUCIA

There is here a goodly array of rare shades in singles, pairs, and blocks, both of the Perkins-Bacon printing and of the De La Rue printings.

St. Vincent

There is amongst other gems a fine copy of the
1/- lilac-rose, two of the 5/-, watermarked Star,
and two of the 4d on 1/- vermilion   The early
perforation varieties, and the surcharges from 1880
onwards, are all in the pink of condition

.

Straits Settlements

Here we find several M S surcharges, including
the 2 on 1½ M S , and a nice lot of the scarcer
types of the printed surcharges, and a pair of the
no surcharge

Of the stamps overprinted " B " for use in *Bangkok*
there is a good show.   The 32c in black on 2a yellow
(wmk Elephant's Head) is represented both unused
and used   The 30c. claret and 96c grey (wmk
Crown C C.) are both shewn unused

In a fairly extensive collection of the stamps
overprinted for the various Native States, it is difficult
to select items for special mention without entering
upon a mere catalogue   The very rare 1c. yellow
and 4c rose of the 1881-83 issue of *Sunger Ujong* are,
however, worth special mention

Tasmania.

The crude first stamps of " Van Diemen's Land,"
and, indeed, the whole of the issues of this colony,
fill a very fine album.   The first 1d is here in a
reconstructed sheet and a number of duplicates, and
four unused.   There is also a good show of the 4d
of the same period.   The later stamps include some
of the rare perforation and roulette varieties

TRANSVAAL

Here we have a very nice lot, but not calling for notable mention, except, perhaps, the fine block of four, used, of the V R red and the *tête bêche* pair of the 1/- unused

TRINIDAD

This island colony is very strongly shown. Large blocks of the first issue engraved and printed by Messrs. Perkins, Bacon & Co , are followed by a nice lot of the stamps lithographed in the colony shewing all stages of the impressions from the finest clear prints to the impressions shewing hardly any of the lines of the background, and including the cartridge paper varieties

There is also an unused copy of the 1/- no watermark, bright mauve, perforated 13

The rare *Lady M'Leod* stamp, which had been issued in 1847 for use on letters conveyed by the steamer of that name trading between San Fernando and Port of Spain, is represented by an unused copy and two used copies on envelopes

TURKS ISLANDS

There are four copies of the rare 1/- prune, complete panes of the $\frac{1}{2}$d surcharge, a strip of six of the " $2\frac{1}{2}$ " on 1d , and a block of four of the " $2\frac{1}{2}$ " on 1/- blue, shewing two of the scarce types.

VICTORIA

Many of the choice items in this colony's stamps came from the Bullock Collection (purchased 1892), to which reference has already been made

There are some choice strips of the first type in scarce shades, eight shades of the *fine background* 2d., and a block of the 3d. first printing, and a single and a pair unused of the 3d., perforated 12.

The plates of the Queen on Throne type have been reconstructed.

Among other rarities there is a beautiful copy in fine colour of the 6d. orange, with beaded oval, for a copy of which stamp I recently paid a record price at the sale of the Mirabaud Collection. There are also three unused and four used copies of the 5/- on yellow paper.

The collection also contains two unused copies of the rare Registration stamp, and four unused copies of the Too Late stamp.

Virgin Islands.

These quaint stamps are shewn in singles, blocks, and sheets. There is a complete sheet of the 1d, watermarked Crown C.C., and the 1d. green of 1866 is included with compound perforation 15x12. Only two or three copies are known of this last-named stamp.

Western Australia.

4d. blue, error—frame inverted.

This colony is represented in particularly fine style. Its gems have come partly from the Bullock Collection (1892), and partly from an exhibit at the Paris International Philatelic Exhibition in the *Palais des Arts Libéraux* in the Champs de Mars, in September, 1892

The Avery copy of the 4d with inverted Swan is probably the finest copy extant of this excessively rare stamp   Sir William purchased it from Mr W. P Rodd, of Hamburg, in 1895

I well remember the day on which he secured this stamp   He was just setting out for the Riviera when it arrived, and he had very little time to catch his train   He rushed into my office on his way to Charing Cross to ask me all about it and what it was worth   He clutched me by the arm, and almost carried me off with him into the train, and on the way to Cannon Street we discussed this very fine new acquisition, of which he was always justifiably proud

In this colony the collection shews the 1/- salmon, which is a rare shade, and a large number of shades of the 1/- brown   Of the roulettes there are the 2d on Indian red, and four of the 4d blue, with the roulettes shewing perfectly all round the stamps

Of the 2d , imperforate, on red there are three pairs and ten singles unused, and three pages of used copies, ranging from the earliest impressions to the latest, the last shewn being one impression which is almost completely undecipherable.   The 6d bronze include four unused and a pair used on envelope, and a number of used copies.

In the 1860 series there are seventy-two 2d , sixteen 4d., and eight 6d , and a very fine lot of the roulettes of all values

1861   There are two singles and a pair unused of the 4d. vermilion, perforated 14-16, six unused specimens of the 6d purple on blued paper, and a pair and three singles of the 1/- deep green, unused.

Sir William had a particular fancy for the 2d. error of colour in the watermarked Crown C C series of 1865.   This is the 2d. in mauve (the colour of the 6d), instead of in yellow.   Consequently, he purchased every one he was offered.   The collection contains no fewer than six unused and two used.

The Avery Collection.

Part II—Foreign Countries

Timbres d'affranchissement pour le
l'intérieur du C

Les Écussons doivent être coupés et collés sur l'autre
Deux Écussons réunis, sont nécessaires pour l'affra
autre commune du canton.
Un seul Écusson affranchit pour l'intérieur de la

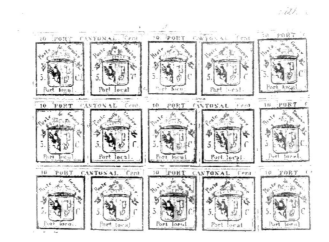

Switzerland.
The "Double Geneva"

Argentine Republic

Of the rare Buenos Ayres " Ship " issues there are three vertical pairs of the DOS PS (2 pesos) blue, in mint state, about half-a-dozen of the TRES PS (3 pesos) green, two CUATO PS (4 pesos) scarlet, and two CINCO PS (5 pesos) yellow, unused

The general issues are practically complete up to 1890 and include some nice pairs and blocks.

Austrian Italy

The lover of old Europeans would be charmed with the display of these stamps in perfect mint blocks of four, including the very valuable 45 centes

Belgium

There is a corner left-hand block of the 10c first issue, unused, twelve of the 1850 10c. brown, and eight of the 20c. blue, " with frame " and side margins of the sheet, also a good strong collection of the other issues

Brazil

The early issues of this country, which was the first to follow Rowland Hill's plan of prepaying postage by means of stamps, make a very interesting show. There are, amongst other items, two sets of the 180, 300, and 600 reis, with slanting figures.

Colombia.

The multitudinous issues for this country and its departments provide a very wide and fascinating field for research without a great expenditure Sir William Avery had a liking for these curious issues, and his collection contains nice pairs in the two *Granada Confederation* series and several beautiful pages of the first issues for the *United States of New Granada,* including used pairs and strips. There is also a very fine copy of the error 50c red of 1863.

There are here, as in other of the American countries, numbers of varieties to be worked out by the specialist.

The rare first types of *Antioquia* are represented by some brilliant copies, and there is a set of the *Cali* provisionals on the grey-blue paper, stamps which are very rarely met with except in the great collections.

DOMINICAN REPUBLIC.

Of both values in the two rare first issues there are several copies and a reconstructed sheet of the ½ real black on rose, wove paper, and 1 real black on green, laid paper. There is a fine lot of the upright oblong stamps of 1866-74, including some sheets and the rare 1 real on blue paper with the inscriptions omitted.

ITALY AND ITALIAN STATES.

The unused 3 lire stamp.

The first issue of *Tuscany* on greyish blue paper includes some blocks for the *connoisseur* of postage stamps. There is an unused block of four of the 1 soldo, and an unused single copy. The 2 soldi is represented by three unused and a pair used. Of the 60 crazie brick-red on azure, of 1852, there are no fewer than two unused and three used.

The 1853 issue on watermarked paper is complete,
and includes two unused and five used of the 1 soldo
yellow buff.

In the next issue (1860) we find a very fine unused
copy of the rarity, the 3 lire yellow, and a used copy.

Naples ½ tornese.   Block of eight used on entire envelope.

In *Naples* there are five copies of the ½ tornese
blue of the "Arms" type of November, 1860, and one
unused of the "Cross" type of December, 1860. The
used copies of the latter include three singles, a pair,
and a block of eight on original cover.

The "King Ferdinand" or "Bomba" issues for
Sicily, which are now being so much sought after by
the student of "retouches," are represented by a fine
array of half sheets, including the 2, 5, and 50gr.
There is a block of six of the 20gr., containing the
rare retouch.

The very interesting *Sardinia* impressed letter
sheets which were used to collect the Government tax

on letters conveyed by carriers and others as early as
1818 are represented by several entire letter sheets,
and there is a choice block of fifteen of the 40c rose
of 1851 issue

The general issues of *Italy*, while of considerable
interest, present no particularly inaccessible items
The collection is practically complete in all the issues.

FRANCE.

Of the first " Ceres " issue of this country, which is
a favourite with specialists, there are mint blocks of
four, including the 15 centimes yellow-green on
green, and the 1 franc vermilion   There are choice
single copies af the 1 franc in the scarce orange shade,
and singles and pairs used on the entire envelopes of
this and other values

Of the varieties in pairs there are some rare items.
A strip of three of the 10c, 1849-50, shewing *tête bêche*,
a pair of the 1 franc 1853-60, Emperor's head,
imperforate, and *tête bêche*, and three pairs of the
1872-75 Ceres type, shewing the 10c and 15c values
se tenant, are some of the gems which attract one's
attention in what must, for the purposes of this
souvenir, be but a casual examination of this collection

In the French colonial stamps we find complete
panes of *Zanzibar* of twenty-five, shewing all the types
of the " 5," " 10," " 25," " 50," and " 1 Fr "
surcharges, the two types *se tenant* of the 15 on 25c of
Majunga, and a very extensive range of other items,
many of which are of considerable rarity, including
sheets shewing types of such colonies as *New
Caledonia*. The rare *Reunions* include the first issue
30 cents with one of the type-set ornaments reversed, a
variety not mentioned in the British catalogues, but
one which is recognised and illustrated in the *Catalogue
Officiel de la Société Française de Timbrologie.*

GERMANY

Bavaria —A good collection of these stamps, including some complete sheets of the early issues and the 6 kreuzer brown, all in a condition that is rarely to be found except when one is fortunate enough to be able to procure the specimens from a large old collection

Brunswick —A block of four of the ¼ silbergroschen black on brown, with full gum and in every way perfect, is an item the lover of old Europeans can appreciate There are also a pair and a single of the ½ sgr. black on green *perces en arc* and two of the 1 gr. on yellow, one of which is an exceptional copy and came from the Ehrenbach collection.

Mecklenburg-Schwerin — Amongst these stamps may be noted two unused ¼ schilling red, rouletted 11½, and three used.

Oldenburg —There are some very choice blocks, including a block of nine ⅓ groschen and a block of 15 of the ¹⁄₃₀ thaler, five used copies of the 3 groschen black on yellow, and eight copies of the rare ⅓ groschen of 1859

Saxony —Of the 3 pf, 1850, there are six copies, including four unused , a pair and single, both mint, of the rare error, ½ ngr on pale blue , some very beautiful mint blocks of the ½, 1, and 2 neugroschen, and six copies of the 2 ngr *deep blue* unused

Thurn and Taxis —The counts of Thurn and Taxis, almost from time immemorial, held the monopoly of the posts over a great part of the continent of Europe, and the stamps issued, bearing the name Thurn and Taxis, served, between 1852 and 1867, large districts

which now form part of the German Empire   Of the
stamps for the southern district served by the Thurn
and Taxis administration, there is a strip of three
of the 3 silbergroschen, a strip of three of the 6 sgr ,
and a pair of the 9 sgr., all unused.   There is also a
pair of the 3 sgr on blue, unused.

Wurtemburg —The most notable items here are
the brilliant mint specimens of the first issue 6 kreuzer
and 9 kreuzer

Greece.

This portion of the collection is highly specialised,
and was originally formed by Lieut. Napier, from
whom Sir William Avery purchased it, since when he
has scarcely added anything of importance.   There is
a beautiful array of blocks and shades arranged
according to the printings.

Hawaii

In this grand philatelic country, so rich in the great
rarities of our hobby, we find three of the
" Missionaries," as the stamps of the first type are
known.   These are, of course, of first rarity   Mr
Henry J Crocker, in his excellent monograph on
Hawaiian Numerals, tells how the popular term
" Missionary " became applied to this issue.   It
"arose from the fact that nearly all the copies which
have been found were on the correspondence from the
missionaries in the Hawaiian Islands to their relatives
and friends in the New England States and California.
To the custom of preserving the letters in the
envelopes, and keeping them as cherished re-
membrances from the absent ones, we owe *the few
specimens that are known of this rare issue* "

The 13 cents " Missionary " stamp, of which both types are included in the Avery collection, is a peculiar denomination.   In discussing the variety inscribed " H I. & U.S. " at the top, Mr Crocker says that these initials, representing " Hawaiian Islands and United States," would go to prove, even at this early date (1852), some arrangement must have existed by which the 13 cent stamp paid not only the 5 cent rate of Hawaiian postage, but a 6 cent rate of the United States and a ship's toll of 2 cents

" These stamps " [inscribed " H.I. & U S."], Mr Crocker says, " are of considerable rarity, being second only to the 2 cents in that respect "

There are in the collection a number of unusual sheets of the plain border numerals, which issues are much rarer than the catalogue quotations would seem to suggest   The errors—

  " HA ———— " ,

  " I " of " INTER " missing ,

  " S " of " POSTAGE " missing.—

are here, and there are two sheets of the 2 cents on laid paper, block of four, printed *tête bêche*, of the 1 cent on blue wove paper, and two sheets of ten   The 1 cent blue on bluish is represented unused, and the 2 cents blue on bluish, used.

MEXICO

All the issues of the first republic are strongly represented with a variety of overprints of the names of postal districts and the dates, and a good selection of the stamps without any overprint, including copies of the 3 centavos brown of 1864-66   There is also a good range of the Gothic overprints, Mexico   The second republic issues, except for the " Anotado " overprints, are well represented, including the errors In the later issues some of the high values are shewn in nice mint pairs   All through this country's stamps we find a number of uncatalogued varieties to delight the specialist in this country, the stamps of which are peculiarly interesting as reflecting the thrilling history of the "coming" country of America.

In the local issues of Mexico there is a particularly fine lot of *Guadalajaras*, with most of the varieties of paper, including several pairs   Chiapas, too, is represented by several copies, including one on entire original

PARAGUAY

There are some nice blocks of the early surcharges and of the "official" overprints.   As in all the South American countries, the collection is very strong in all these issues

PERU.

There are here some nice pieces, including the Pacific Steam Navigation Company's stamps.   Of the first Government issues there is one of the error $\frac{1}{2}$ peso, rose-red, and two shades of the stamp in the correct colour, yellow   There are two of the 1862-63, with the arms sideways, and a nice general lot of all the subsequent issues, including many of the local overprints

PORTUGAL

The issues are fairly complete, including the varieties, the straight, and the curly hair sets.   There is a complete sheet of the 25 reis of 1856.   The colonial issues complete a bulky volume, including, among the rarer pieces, a very fine copy of the 5 reis, imperforate, Azores of 1868; three of the small surcharge on the 150 reis blue perforated $12\frac{1}{2}$, and a pair of the 40 reis blue, shewing Cape Verde and Mozambique issues *se tenant.*

ROUMANIA—MOLDAVIA.

Unique pair of the 27 paras.

Here the Avery collection stands unrivalled in the possession of the first circular type. These stamps, as the experienced collector is fully aware, are luxuries, their extreme rarity having placed them in the first rank of philatelic gems. For these stamps Sir William had quite a special fondness, as witness the number he acquired of stamps which even the wealthy collector is generally content with single copies.

There are three magnificent singles of the 27 paras, with red and blue postmarks, *and a pair*, the latter being an acquisition of which its late owner was justifiably proud.

Of the *six* copies of the 54 paras, one is on the entire original envelope.

There are *four* of the rarest stamp in the series, the 81 paras, including an exceptionally large unused copy with wide margins all round, an unique copy, which came from the Westoby collection.

Of the 108 paras there are six specimens, one unused and one with very large margins used on entire.

It must seem surprising that even a man of Sir William's keenness and wealth should have been able

to amass so many of the very limited number of copies
known of these stamps   He was, however, more than
ordinarily interested in them.

On one occasion—it was. I think, the 26th May,
1896—he bought from Mons. Dorsan Astruc three
complete sets of these rare stamps, and I have the
memorandum which gives two thousand pounds sterling
as the price paid for the twelve stamps

SWITZERLAND.

An extract from the Minutes of the Council of State
of the Canton of *Zurich* shows that the Postal
Administration of the Canton was one of the first
foreign administrations to recognise the great benefits
of the British Postal System, introduced in 1840   As
early as August 13th, 1842, a proposal was laid before
the Council, and the Zurich stamps were in use by
. March, 1843.

Of these rare Zurich stamps there are six of the
4 rappen, unused and used on entires, and a whole
page of the 6 rappen value.

The "double *Geneva*" stamp 5c + 5c. black on
yellow-green paper, consists, as the name suggests, of
two stamps joined together, and which were to be
used thus for the single letter rate on letters going from
one Canton to another, while, if cut apart, each half
served for a single letter whose destination was within
the limits of the Canton of issue.

The stamps were printed in sheets of 50 double
stamps, and the top left-hand corner block of six
"doubles" and three halves with top marginal
inscriptions, which I reproduce (page 40) from the
Avery albums, is certainly one of the greatest
treasures of the collection.

Some of my readers may have seen the Avery display of Switzerland at the 1906 London International Exhibition, where this celebrated block of double Genevas was voted one of the finest things in the Exhibition There can be no question that this is the finest item in any collection of Swiss stamps I myself sold it to Sir William Avery a good many years ago

There are eight other double Genevas, and four halves used as 5 cent stamps

One of the most admired pieces in the late Mons. Mirabaud's collection of Switzerland, and illustrated in his sumptuous work " *The Postage Stamps of Switzerland, 1843-1862*," was a fine top marginal block with parts of the first two rows of the stamp known as the 5 cent " Large eagle " Sir William's collection contains one piece shewing the two top rows (twenty stamps) complete with the full top marginal inscriptions, another grand item not to be matched in any other collection, the nearest being the fourteen stamps in the Mirabaud block.

The stamp of *Basle*, which was the third of the Swiss Cantons to use postage stamps, is also a rare stamp, represented by as many as twelve copies, including unused and used on entire envelopes

Of the stamps popularly known as the " *Vaud* " issues, but which actually belong to the period of transition from the separate postal administrations of the various Cantons to the central control of the Confederation, there are six of rare 4 cents. One is unused, and I illustrate a pair used on original envelope. A page is filled with the 5 cents, black and red, of January, 1850.

Timbres d'affranchissement pour les lettres au dessous de 1 once.
Dans l'intérieur du Canton de Genève.

Les Ecussons doivent être coupés et collés sur l'adresse des lettres qu'on veut affranchir.
Un seul Ecusson suffit pour affranchir une lettre adressée d'une Commune à une autre Commune du Canton.

Lith. Schmid à Genève.

Used pair of the 4c. " Poste Locale."

Of the 5 cents POSTE LOCALE (Neúchatel) of August, 1805, one unused and two used copies are included.

There are also very fine reconstructed plates of the first stamps of the Federal Administration inscribed ORTS-POST, and those inscribed POSTE-LOCALE with and without frame.

Both the Cantonal and general issues of Switzerland are so finely displayed that it is not easy to select items for mention beyond the very notable ones briefly referred to. Practically everything is here in a condition in which these beautiful issues are extremely difficult to procure.

UNITED STATES.

In the section devoted to the Postmasters' stamps, issued prior to the introduction of adhesive stamps by the United States Government, there are some notable rarities.

There is a 5 cents *Baltimore*, frequently called "Buchanan" from the name of the Postmaster which appears on the stamp. This is on the entire original envelope.

Another fine specimen is the *Brattleboro* on entire original.

The Millbury Postmaster's Stamp.

Rarer still is the *Millbury* local, which is also on the entire.

There are no fewer than seven copies of the *St. Louis* Postmaster's stamps, of which two are on pelure paper.

Of the regular stamps of the United States Government, there is a very large and beautiful collection, comprising the 24c. grey-lilac of 1857, imperforate, and brilliant copies of the 24c. and 30c. *premières gravures* of August, 1861. In the very popular and pretty 1869 issue, all three of the rare inverted centres are included, viz., the 15c., 24c., and 30c., the last named being a perfect unused copy, exceedingly rare in this condition, only a very few copies being known unused.

Of the "grille" embossing, there are many varieties, and all the later issues are shewn in splendid array of mint and used copies and some very choice blocks.

CONFEDERATE STATES.

This is one of the series of postal issues for which Sir William had a very great partiality, and his collection of the Confederate locals was undoubtedly the finest in this country.

Of the *Athens* (Georgia) stamp, there are three original envelopes bearing used copies shewing the types in pairs.

The Baton Rouge Stamp.

The *Baton Rouge* (Louisiana) stamps include the error "McCormack" on the 2c. green on original envelope, and the 5c. carmine and green with the same error.

The *Danville* (Virginia), and *Goliad* (Texas), are both used, and the *Lenoir* (North Carolina), is unused.

The Stamp of Goliad, Texas.

The *Livingston* (Alabama) 5 cents blue is illustrated in this booklet from the superb copy on entire in the collection.

Livingston (Alabama). U.S.A.

The Madison Stamp with CENTS spelt correctly.

The *Madison* stamp, too, is illustrated. This is an extremely rare stamp, and is very well authenticated by documents which I acquired along with the collection. The stamp is certainly one of the very rarest of the Confederate locals. Prior to the discovery of this copy only one copy was known, that being one in the Philbrick collection, which was the variety with the error of spelling, CNETS for CENTS, from which the familiar catalogue illustrations have descended, leading occasionally to the erroneous impression that all the varieties in the setting were so spelt.

The particular specimen with the correct spelling, which I illustrate from the Avery collection, has a curious and not uninteresting history. It was obtained by a medical practitioner in Washington. He says that he received the envelope "from a patient who made a careful search for old letters upon my request. It (the Madison envelope) had been continuously in the possession of my patient, a relative of the original writer, and a sister of the person addressed, for over

thirty-four years.   .   Since received in this city
(Washington), in the mail, February, '61, that
envelope has been in the hands of only the addressee,
his sister, who had it some thirty-four years, and
myself   I agreed to part with it only after
the death of my patient   .   '

Of the *Mobile* (Alabama), there are four unused 2c.
black and a pair and two singles of the 5c blue.

There are several of *Nashville* (Tennessee), and
two pairs shewing types *se tenant* of the *Tellico Plains*
(Tennessee) stamps, besides many of the other
Confederate locals.

URUGUAY.

This is a good specialised collection, covering most
of the numerous issues very fully, and including some
fine copies of the " Diligencias " and the " Montevideo"
types

(Temporary.)
To be posted at the HOUSE OF LORDS only.
Post Paid —**ONE PENNY.**—Weight not to exceed oz.

Great Britain, 1840.   The House of Lords Envelope.

SPECIALITY ·
NEW ISSUES

W. H. PECKITT,

47, STRAND, LONDON, W.C.

DEALER IN
RARE STAMPS

NEW ISSUE SERVICE.

THE difficulty Collectors used to experience in keeping pace with new issues of postage stamps emanating from all quarters of the Globe has been entirely done away with by the introduction of my New Issue Service Clients joining this service can have all New Issues of British Colonial Stamps, as they are imported by me at an uniform charge of

TEN PER CENT. OVER FACE VALUE.

This enables the private Collector to keep his collection up-to-date with a minimum of trouble and expense It is a distinct saving on the old system of buying these new issues promiscuously at amounts which were rarely less than 100 per cent over face for the low values, and as much as 50 per cent and 33⅓ per cent on the high values

The advantages peculiar to my New Issue Service may be summed up as —

> ECONOMY (10 per cent on actual total face value from fractions to pounds)
>
> COMPLETE DISTRIBUTIONS (All I import are faithfully distributed regardless of actual or prospective rises in market value)
>
> SIMPLE ACCOUNTS.
>
> REGULAR AND PROMPT DELIVERY
>
> SCOPE (British Colonies, either in the simple form of King's Heads only, or with varieties of shades, perforation and paper)

FULL EXPLANATORY CIRCULAR SENT FREE ON APPLICATION

W. H. PECKITT,

47, STRAND, LONDON, W.C.

Telephone—GERRARD 3204
Telegrams and Cables—" PECKITT, LONDON '

THE AVERY COLLECTION.

HAVING recently purchased this, the largest general collection of Postage Stamps ever sold outright, for the cash price of £24,500, I am prepared to send portions of the collection on approval, as usual, to responsible collectors.

RARE STAMPS (British and Foreign).

MY general stock is particularly strong in rarities of British Colonial and Foreign Stamps, rare stamps being an important speciality of my business. As a ready purchaser for cash of highly specialised collections, I am constantly having through my hands rarities of the first and second order, but always in the finest possible condition. Specialists should therefore inspect my stocks, and send me lists of their wants.

MEDIUM STAMPS.

ALTHOUGH rare stamps are a speciality of my business, every attention is given to the needs of customers for the medium and the commoner classes of stamps, and the uniform feature of my stock books is the high standard of condition maintained This is a factor of the first importance to the collector who is expecting his stamp album to be a sound and profitable investment

PACKETS, SETS, ALBUMS, ACCESSORIES, &c.

THE requirements of the beginner are catered for in Packets ranging in price from 1/- to £20, and in a comprehensive series of sets Albums of all grades and all the requisites of the stamp collector can be supplied on the most moderate terms A list of Packets, Sets, Albums, &c , will be sent post free on application.

THE MELVILLE STAMP BOOKS

THIS popular series of books on the stamps of favourite countries aims at enabling every Collector to form a standard reference library of books on stamp collecting, at the uniform price of 6d. per book (post free, 7d) The books are copiously illustrated, and contain *complete* check lists and good bibliographical indices, as well as neatly printed gummed labels to save writing in the stamp album The books already published in this series are :—

    1 GREAT BRITAIN Line Engraved Stamps
    2 BRITISH CENTRAL AFRICA AND NYASALAND PROTECTORATE.
    3 UNITED STATES POSTAGE STAMPS, 1847-1869
    4 GAMBIA.   5. NEVIS.   6 HOLLAND
    7. TONGA (Friendly Islands).
    8 BRITISH NEW GUINEA AND PAPUA

All the above are 6d. each, post free, 7d A second series of eight books will be published at intervals during the year 1910, and will be supplied post free to subscribers at 4/2 the series of eight books.

W. H. PECKITT,

47, STRAND, LONDON, W C

Telephone—Gerrard 3204   Telegrams and Cables—" Peckitt, London '

CPSIA information can be obtained
at www.ICGtesting.com
Printed in the USA
LVHW081120130323
741356LV00037B/429